Becoming a Woman
God Can Use

BY JUDITH COUCHMAN

Bible Studies

Daring to Be Different: A Study on Deborah
Becoming a Woman God Can Use: A Study on Esther
Entrusting Your Dreams to God: A Study on Hannah
Choosing the Joy of Obedience: A Study on Mary
Celebrating Friendship
His Gentle Voice (Bible study in the book)
Designing a Woman's Life Bible Study
Why Is Her Life Better Than Mine?
If I'm So Good, Why Don't I Act That Way?
Getting a Grip on Guilt

Books

The Shadow of His Hand
His Gentle Voice
A Garden's Promise
The Woman Behind the Mirror
Shaping a Woman's Soul
Designing a Woman's Life
Lord, Please Help Me to Change
Lord, Have You Forgotten Me?

Compilations

Encouragement for the Heart
Psalm 23
Amazing Grace
Voices of Faith
Promises for Spirit-Led Living
Cherished Thoughts about Friendship
Cherished Thoughts about Love
Cherished Thoughts about Prayer
Breakfast for the Soul
One Holy Passion

Life Messages of Great Christians Series

His Redeeming Love (Jonathan Edwards)
The Way of Faith (Martin Luther)
Growing in Grace (John Wesley)
Called to Commitment (Watchman Nee)
The Promise of Power (Jamie Buckingham)
Only Trust Him (Dwight L. Moody)
For Me to Live Is Christ (Charles Spurgeon)
Growing Deeper with God (Oswald Chambers)
Dare to Believe (Smith Wigglesworth)
Anywhere He Leads Me (Corrie ten Boom)
Loving God with All Your Heart (Andrew Murray)
A Very Present Help (Amy Carmichael)

WOMEN OF FAITH℠
BIBLE STUDY SERIES

Women of the Bible

Becoming a Woman
God Can Use

A Study on Esther

Judith Couchman

Foreword by Thelma Wells

GRAND RAPIDS, MICHIGAN 49530 USA

ZONDERVAN™

Becoming a Woman God Can Use
Formerly titled *Esther*
Copyright © 1999 by Women of Faith, Inc.

Judith Couchman, General Editor

Requests for information should be addressed to:

Zondervan, *Grand Rapids, Michigan 49530*

ISBN 0-310-24782-9

Interior design by Sherri Hoffman

Printed in the United States of America

03 04 05 06 /❖ CH/ 10 9 8 7 6 5 4

For all who enter the Esther house
at Praise Mountain

Contents

Acknowledgments

*M*any thanks to Ann Spangler at Zondervan for giving me the opportunity to write about my biblical role model, Esther, and to Lori Walburg for her careful editing. Also to Charette Barta, Win Couchman, Madalene Harris, Karen Hilt, and Nancy Lemons — all women who are available to God, especially through prayer. And to my beloved mother, who sticks by me when I risk it all.

Foreword

*G*od can take a displaced, orphaned teenager and raise her up to save a nation. God can use a frightened, insecure young girl to accomplish a great mission. He did it in the life of Queen Esther. He wants to do it in your life.

I marvel at how theatrical God is as he orchestrates the events in our lives. He controls the drama of our lives by creating the characters, preparing the backdrop, developing the setting, planning the plot, directing the scenes, affecting the finale, and announcing the curtain call. Esther's life is a prime example.

A Jewish orphan being raised in Persia by a single man, Esther didn't have a clue about what was going to happen in her life. Perhaps she would have laughed if you had told her she would save her people from destruction. *How could that be? I'm a lowly orphan girl!* But God knew when, where, how, what time, to whom, and why Esther was born. Her innate qualities of intelligence, respect, faith, humility, creativity, courage, flexibility, submission, obedience, long-suffering, and leadership were a part of her DNA from the moment she was conceived. God needed a character like Esther to carry out his plan.

As you study this fascinating and charming girl being transformed into a woman God can use, you may be able to put yourself in her place at least part of the time. I did.

Esther was raised by a surrogate parent, just like me.

Esther was displaced in a country where her heritage was frowned on, just like me.

Esther was educated in the traditions and customs of her environment, just like me.

Esther revered the God of her ancestors, just like me.

Esther feared being ignored or rejected, just like me.

Esther was protected from hurt, harm, and danger, just like me.

Esther was called by God to do a special work for his kingdom, just like me.

Esther's assignment by God was completed and honored, just like I want mine to be.

It may be hard for you to imagine yourself doing a work like Esther. But God didn't call you to do what Esther did. He calls you to be a woman he can use. A woman who will love him and give him glory. A woman who has faith in him and believes he will keep his promises.

God has a plan for you. He created you to have fellowship with him, to love him with all your heart, and to acknowledge him so he can direct your paths. Everything you've experienced in your life from the moment of your birth to this very moment has been preparing you to play out your part in life's drama. God wants you to allow him to provide the script, rehearse you, produce you, manage you, direct you, and move you through the finale to the final curtain call when he takes you home. He realizes that when your life's drama is acted out in his brilliance, you and the world around you will never be the same.

Mordecai asked the question, "Who knows but that you have come to royal position for such a time as this?" (Esther 4:14). That question is asked of you too. Remember, you are never exempt from the responsibilities God has called you to. God can change your impossibilities into possibilities. God will never give you an assignment you cannot handle.

Who would have thought that a little black girl born to a crippled teenager in the segregated South would someday speak to over one million people? As a young girl, I never imagined it. But God had a plan.

As you grow closer to God during this Bible study, listen for the still, small voice of God whispering in your ear things he wants you to do. Don't worry about how you will do them. God will show you how in due season. Stay alert and don't be manipulated by the enemy. What God ordains, he sustains. He will take your assignments and work them out to a glorious solution, just as he did for Esther.

— *Thelma Wells*

About This Study

*E*veryone loves a captivating story. It can prompt laughter, tears, nods of the head, even thoughtful silence. Best of all, a good story teaches us how to live better. It doles out guidelines, points to pitfalls, and inspires us toward heart-changing action. It infuses the ordinary with meaning and the tragic with truth.

In this Women of Faith discussion guide you'll explore one of those poignant stories. Through the life of Esther, a biblical woman with an intriguing dilemma, you'll learn how God can work in the world, in the lives of his people, and in your circumstances. Each of the six sessions unfolds her story, compares it to yours, and initiates a group discussion that will invoke spiritual growth and life-related applications.

To most effectively utilize this discussion guide with your group, consider organizing your time as follows.

BEFORE THE GROUP SESSION

Before attending a meeting, take time alone to evaluate your life and prepare for the next group discussion. During this time read and ponder the following sections of the discussion guide.

- *Opening Narrative.* Each week you'll be ushered into another chapter of Esther's story. This fiction narrative introduces her unusual circumstances and helps you envision how Esther felt, and perhaps what she did, as the events around her unfolded. It can get you thinking about the story before the group assembles, and whet your appetite for what happens next.
- *Setting the Stage.* Based on Esther's story and the session's theme, think about your life. The questions and suggested activities can help you consider the following: How am I doing in this area? How do I feel about it? What do I want to do or change? How does this affect my spiritual life? Be honest with yourself and God, asking him to teach you through Esther's story.

The heart of this guide focuses on gathering together for discussion and encouragement. It allows time to study the Bible, apply its truths to your lives, and pray together. Of course, you can add whatever else fits the nature of your group, such as time for a "coffee klatch" or "catching up on each other's lives." Whatever you decide, reserve about an hour for the next four sections.

- *Discussing Esther's Story.* In this section read and discuss a biblical passage that captures the remarkable events of Esther's life. Though the discussion centers on the facts of God's Word, at times you'll read between the lines and suggest people's feelings, motivations, and character qualities to gain insights to their actions. Still, you can answer these questions without compromising the biblical text.

  To best manage this discussion time, you can follow these steps:

  1. Ask one woman to read out loud the fiction narrative, if it seems appropriate. If not, skip this step.
  2. As a group read aloud the Bible passage stated at the beginning of the section. Take turns reading verses so each woman participates.
  3. Discuss the questions together, consulting specific verses from the text as needed.

- *Behind the Scenes.* This section provides background information related to the biblical text. It enlightens the story's culture and history, and helps you answer the discussion questions. You can refer to this section as you discuss Esther's story.

- *Sharing Your Story.* How does Esther's story apply to your life? As a group you can answer the questions in this section, relating the events of her life to your own and uncovering nuggets of practical application. These questions target group sharing rather than personal contemplation.

- *Prayer Matters.* To conclude your session use these ideas to guide the group in prayer, especially focusing on individual needs.

AFTER A MEETING

Since spiritual growth doesn't end with your small group gathering, try these suggestions to extend learning into the next week and encourage one-on-one relationships. However, these sections are optional, depending on your interest and schedule.

- *After Hours.* These activities help apply the lesson's principles to everyday life. You can complete them with a friend or by yourself.
- *Words to Remember.* After you return home, memorize the selected Bible verse for encouragement and guidance.

In addition, the back of this book presents a Leader's Guide to help your group's facilitator pilot the discussion. To insure that everyone contributes to the conversation, it's best to keep the group at six to eight participants. If the membership increases, consider splitting into smaller groups during the discussion times and gathering together for the concluding prayer.

However you organize the meeting, keep the emphasis on discussion — sharing ideas, needs, and questions, rather than striving for a consensus of opinion. That's the pleasure of a good story. It stimulates thinking and reflects our inner selves, so along with Esther we can become women of faith.

— Judith Couchman, General Editor

Introduction

As a girl attending Sunday school, I made Esther the woman of my dreams. She was brave, beautiful, and a true heroine. She captured the king's heart and saved her people from destruction. When her cousin Mordecai proclaimed, "Who knows but that you have come to royal position for such a time as this?" (Esther 4:14), my heart thumped. I wanted to become a woman for such a time as this — a woman God could use.

The problem, however, was that Esther seemed perfect. I was not.

Through the years I nearly gave up my desire to grow into God's woman of purpose. I frequently landed in the wrong place at the wrong time, goofed up and gave into sin, and pursued what I wanted when I wanted it. How could God use me? Why would he want to?

Eventually as an adult I stumbled back onto Esther's story, and what I discovered there surprised me. Esther wasn't perfect. In fact, today she'd create a religious stir. She lived in a pagan city rather than Jerusalem; she entered a harem with its disregard for monogamy; she concealed her ancestry; she married a man outside the Jewish race. None of these actions represented God's desire for his people, but when she determined to risk her life for his sake, he profoundly used her for his purposes.

This cheered me. It's not that I believed I could deliberately sin and be used by God. It's that despite my failings, in spite of unfavorable circumstances, God would employ me in his service if my heart turned toward him. If I learned to obey him now, rather than getting stuck in the regrettable past or waiting for some perfect time in the distant future. If I began living for his purpose, not mine.

And that's the message of this discussion guide. You don't have to wait for personal or circumstantial perfection to significantly touch others and make a difference for God in the world. Right now, if you're willing to follow him, you can be a woman used by God.

— *Judith Couchman*

Who's in Control?

When life feels out of whack,
God is still working.

*V*ashti smiled at the ornately dressed noblewoman seated next to her and asked, "So, what have you thought of the king's grand party?"

"Magnificent!" the woman exclaimed. "My husband says it has boosted his confidence in King Xerxes and his ability to conquer the Greeks in battle."

"Ah, yes, the Greeks. I almost forgot about them," sighed Vashti.

The noblewoman laughed, but Vashti did not. For half a year her husband had presided over a massive celebration for their kingdom, with princes and paupers traipsing through the palace day and night. Xerxes had explained that before waging war, he wanted to exhibit wealth and strength to his subjects and the world. "It will make our warriors proud and our enemies afraid," he'd said, crossing his arms with satisfaction. But Vashti knew that even without the pending conflict, Xerxes delighted in showing off his power and possessions—and he loved to eat, drink, and be merry.

And that six months was enough to make any wife weary.

Tonight, during the celebration's final banquet, Vashti had distanced herself from the king and his drunken men by entertaining visiting women in the palace. It was a workable feast for her, until halfway through the meal the king's attendants materialized at the banquet door.

"The king commands that you appear at his feast, wearing your royal crown," they announced. Their words murmured through the banquet hall and hushed the queen's chattering guests.

"Why? Why does he need me?" insisted Vashti, but she knew the answer. She was to display herself to the king's rowdy guests.

Vashti paused resolutely, then said, "No, I will not come."

The attendants turned ashen and women gasped in unison, as if an apparition had suddenly entered the great hall. If the queen truly meant those words, they'd banish her from the kingdom.

"But the king has ordered!" spluttered an attendant.

Vashti scanned the room's stricken faces, then replied, "Yes, and I have refused."

The queen turned from the messengers and stared at a silver pitcher on the table, knowing her life had just spun out of control.

Setting the Stage

HOW'S YOUR WORLD?

We may not face a decision as dire as Vashti's, but at one time or another we all pass through times when life careens out of control. Not much progresses as we think it should and everything feels unfair and out of whack.

Before attending the first group discussion, grab a few moments alone and create a picture of your world. Draw a horizontal line toward the bottom of a page to represent the ground on which you stand. Sketch a stick figure of yourself standing on this "ground." On the line with you, draw the things in your life that feel "grounded" and in control. Above you and the ground, draw the things in your life that feel unfair and out of control. Don't just focus on daily circumstances, but also think about long-range dreams and goals.

Ponder your picture. How many things in your life seem out of control? How do you feel about this? Which situations can you affect by changing yourself or your lifestyle? Which ones are truly beyond your control? Write an honest prayer to God about the things you can't control. What do you want to tell him? What would you like him to tell you?

Discussing Esther's Story

A BATTLE OF THE WILLS

The book of Esther opens to a battle of the wills. Queen Vashti commits the unthinkable and refuses the king's request. The arrogant king can't abide her disobedience and rages against it. Who will win? Read chapter one to find out, and consider this: Who's really in control here? The king? The queen? Or an unseen Someone?

Before you begin the discussion, read the Bible text, Esther 1.

1. Xerxes the Great was Persia's sixth king (486–465 B.C.) and one of the wealthiest men in the ancient world. In verses 1–8, why would the book's unnamed author (suggested to be Mordecai) feel compelled to describe the king's ostentatious style?

2. To understand the context of the king's grand party, read the Behind the Scenes section, "A Big, Brawling Bash," on page 24. Why would Vashti's compliance with her husband's six-month celebration be important?

3. Now witness the conflict. Read verses 10–12 again. Some Bible scholars believe the king commanded Vashti to appear unveiled, which invoked scandal even in pagan Persian courts. Others suggest she was to wear only her royal crown, which would have meant unshakable degradation. One commentator explains that at the very least, the king's behavior was "ungentlemanly" and "positively crude." What other factors would have caused Vashti to refuse her husband's request?

4. Based on the circumstances, do you feel Vashti was "right" or "wrong" in her refusal? Why?

5. Though Xerxes wielded tremendous power as king, the laws of the
    Medes and Persians were so immutable, he couldn't override them.
    So the king asked his advisers, "According to the law, what must be
    done to Queen Vashti?" (verse 15). In verses 16–20, does the
    episode's outcome seem fair to you? Why, or why not?

6. What a mess! A drunken king requests an unseemly act. His queen,
    gathering up her dignity, refuses him. She suffers banishment, and
    the law tightens on women in the kingdom. It all looks hopeless and
    hardly redemptive. God seems nowhere in sight. In fact, he is never
    mentioned in the book of Esther. Yet in the background Providence
    is at work. Vashti's downfall leads to Esther's rise in the kingdom.
    The Bible offers no explanation for this irony, but why do you think
    God eventually allowed one woman to profit from another woman's
    misfortune? Explore more than one answer.

Behind the Scenes

A BIG, BRAWLING BASH

Vashti's husband was Xerxes the Great of Persia (Ahasuerus in some Bible translations) and from a pagan viewpoint he possessed much to boast about. The king catapulted Persia to its zenith, ruling the vast territory from India to Ethiopia. His wealth staggered the imagination.

No doubt Xerxes could afford to throw a garish, six-month party, and he wanted everyone to know it. He paraded his fortunes: military weapons and warriors; slaves and artifacts from conquered territories; the gold-encrusted palace and furnishings; and servants, wives, and concubines. Princes from the 127 provinces attended, and as a finale all of the capital city of Susa, from the lowly to the lauded, joined in.

When archaeologists excavated Susa centuries later, they unearthed etched inscriptions about Xerxes that read, "The great king. The king of kings. The king of lands occupied by many races. The king of this great earth." It was this "great king" that Xerxes displayed in his half-year celebration. Because he planned a later military campaign against Greece, the only significant part of the world not under his reign, the king wanted both allies and enemies to recognize his ability to finance and wage war.

Ironically, after all the pompous proceedings, Xerxes lost his battle with Greece.

Sharing Your Story

GOD IN THE SHADOWS

The poet James Russell Lowell wrote, "Behind the dim unknown, / Standeth God within the shadow, / keeping watch above his own." This is the story of Esther. It's also your story. When God seems nowhere in sight, he still controls the world and its events, even the twists in your everyday life.

ESTHER – *Becoming a Woman God Can Use*

1. Pull out a current newspaper and hand a few pages to each group member. According to these pages, what events in the international, national, and/or local news seem out of control? How do you feel about these situations?

2. How about your personal life? Does anything feel out of control there? (You may want to consult your notes from the Setting the Stage section "How's Your World?" on page 20, but share only what feels comfortable to you.) On a whiteboard or easel pad, create a composite list of what seems personally out of whack to group members.

3. What would you like to ask God about these problems?

4. Read Psalm 46. What is God's message to us about out-of-control circumstances? Practically, how can we respond to his words?

5. Based on your group list, how can you take control of the possible and let go of the impossible, offering the uncontrollable to God's care?

6. From the message of Esther 1 and Psalm 46, write a reassuring letter from God to your group, explaining his providential care.

Even when life feels unmanageable, God can still use you in unfavorable circumstances, if you're willing to let him. In fact, he specializes in dropping the miraculous into a mess. So take a deep breath and wait for what God will do.

Prayer Matters

A CIRCLE OF PRAYER

To end today's session, form a circle of prayer. For five minutes, say one-sentence prayers about what feels out of control in (1) the world, (2) your nation, and (3) your lives. To conclude your prayer time, read together Psalm 46:10 in "Words to Remember" on page 27.

ESTHER – *Becoming a Woman God Can Use*

MANAGING THE POSSIBLE

We can't straighten out the world's mess, but we can affect our own lives. So, this week, work on "managing the possible" rather than fretting about what seems impossible.

With a friend: With one partner or a group, "prayer walk" through a place that seems out of control. It could be someone's home, a school, an office building, a neighborhood. As you walk through the area intercede for the people and situations there, waging spiritual warfare and asking God for his redemption in this place.

On your own: Sometimes getting one thing under control helps settle your soul midst the world's chaos. So this week tackle a manageable mess in your life. A junk drawer, a cluttered schedule, an unfinished project, a hurting relationship. Anything that needs straightening out or definable closure. Initiate the action yourself and afterward you'll feel "cleaned out" personally and spiritually. Your corner of the world will be in better shape.

Words to Remember

GOD WILL BE EXALTED

Cease striving and know that I am God,

I will be exalted among the nations,

I will be exalted in the earth.

—Psalm 46:10 (NASB)

Wrong Place, Right Attitude

*You can cultivate the qualities
God can use.*

*A*s Esther scuttled deeper into the marbled room, caught in a crowd of attractive young women, she heard the great doors slam behind them, sealing her fate.

So this is the harem, she thought. *I've heard about the luxury ... the pampering ... the competition for the king's attention. But I never thought I'd see it for myself.* The other new harem members began exploring the room, but Esther stood motionless.

Suddenly a eunuch carrying a gold tray of perfumes brushed by, casting a sly smile over his shoulder as he stopped to steady the load. He turned and briefly surveyed her body, hair to ankles, in one gliding motion. To Esther it seemed like forever.

"Gorgeous," he pronounced, "simply gorgeous."

The eunuch laughed at Esther's startled face and hurried into a huddle of sheerly dressed women by the indoor pool, missing the rising flush in her cheeks. Feeling both flattered and frustrated, Esther stared into the transparent water. She missed her home, and especially her cousin Mordecai, who'd always protected and guided her.

What will I do? she wondered. *My life has vanished.* Entering the king's harem meant she might never return to the bustling world outside the palace gates, even if, like most of these women, she wouldn't be crowned queen to replace Vashti. *Once in the harem, always in the harem,* she recited inwardly, knowing that after the king gathered up beautiful women, they usually became ladies-in-waiting for life.

Yahweh, are you here? Tell me what to do. She waited, but heard only her own sigh.

Suddenly a hand on Esther's shoulder interrupted her thoughts. She looked up into another set of eyes. Assured and admiring, they calmed her.

"I am Hegai," he said. "I'm the one in charge here. Come with me." Grabbing Esther's elbow, he led her past the waters through a golden door.

Setting the Stage

ARE YOU QUALIFIED?

If God said to you, "I'm looking for a woman to help fulfill my plan for the world," would you feel qualified? Probably not. Most of us don't. And most likely, Esther didn't either.

God understands our weakness and inexperience. In fact, he specializes in using unlikely people in his service. He just needs our willingness to make a difference for (and with) him.

Sometime before this week's group session, write a job description that delineates your qualifications for "being a woman God can use to fulfill his plan." Include your weaknesses as well as your strengths. For example, *I tend to stick my foot in my mouth, but I love to read God's Word.* Or, *Speaking publicly scares me, but I'm good at one-to-one friendships.*

When you've completed your "job qualifications," offer them—both strengths and weaknesses—to the Lord in prayer. Express your willingness (or even unwillingness) to be used by God, and ask him to develop in you the character qualities that he needs.

BEAUTY ON PARADE

With Vashti banished from the kingdom, Xerxes needed to fill an important job opening. But how would he find the queen of his dreams? Though the king devised an elaborate plan that served his appetite for gorgeous women, the decision really didn't belong to him. It resided in the heart of God, who kept a young Jewish woman waiting in the harem.

Before you begin the discussion, read the Bible text, Esther 2.

1. Verse one of this chapter claims that Xerxes "remembered Vashti ... and what he had decreed about her." What might this indicate about the king's thoughts regarding his treatment of Vashti?

2. Read about Mordecai in verses 5–11. When the exiled Jews were allowed to return to Jerusalem (Israel), the homeland God intended them to live in, many stayed in Susa (Persia) because they enjoyed the freedom of running their own businesses and accepting government positions. According to verse 21, Mordecai evidently held a political job because he sat near the king's gate. What do these two descriptions of Mordecai (in verses 10–11 and 21–22) reveal about his character?

3. Read the description of a Persian harem in the Behind the Scenes section, "Lost in the Harem," on page 32. For Esther to enter the harem and possibly marry the king violated Jewish laws about morality and marriage to foreigners. Why would Mordecai allow Esther to participate in this beauty parade? Why would he forbid Esther to admit her nationality?

4. In verses 10–18 we learn more about Esther. Do you think her beauty was the only asset that caused people to favor her? Why, or why not?

5. Contemporary women sometimes struggle to accept Esther's circumstances and behavior. At this point do you find any of Esther's story hard to accept, or at least to understand? If so, discuss this with the group.

6. Aspects of Esther's life don't fit the traditional idea of following God's will: she lived with godless people in Susa instead of with God's people in Jerusalem; she concealed her nationality; she participated in harem practices; and she married outside the Jewish race. Yet in the next sessions we'll discover how God uses her. Why would he still use Esther for his purposes, despite these facts?

Behind the Scenes

LOST IN THE HAREM

Persian kings collected not only vast amounts of jewelry, but also great numbers of women. These young virgins were taken from their homes and required to live in a separate building near the palace, called a harem.

Their sole purpose was to serve the king and to await his call for sexual pleasure. They rarely saw the king, and their lives were restricted and boring. If rejected, Esther would be one of many girls the king has seen once and forgotten. But Esther's presence and beauty pleased the king enough that he crowned her queen in place of Vashti. The queen held a more influential position than a concubine, and she was given more freedom than others in the harem. But even as queen, Esther had few rights — especially because she had been chosen to replace a woman who had become too assertive.

—from *The Life Application Bible*,
New International Version

ESTHER — *Becoming a Woman God Can Use*

BUT WHAT ABOUT ME?

In this study book you'll note attitudes and character qualities in Esther that made her a woman God could use. But will these qualities translate to your culture, your circumstances? It's a question to ask throughout these sessions, beginning now.

1. Esther has been ushered into a place she didn't expect (or perhaps choose) to be. Yet she seems to accept her plight and flow with it. How can you determine when to accept or try to change unpleasant circumstances? Explain your answer.

2. So far Esther's life could raise a few orthodox eyebrows, but at the same time, she exhibits qualities God can use in a pagan place. What are they? Write them on the board and discuss why each quality is important to her setting.

3. How would these qualities translate into our culture? Would they be understood and respected by others? Why, or why not?

4. On an index card or small piece of paper, write an unwanted and difficult situation a woman could face today. Hand the scenario to the group's leader. As she reads each description from group members, discuss how the "Esther qualities" you listed in question two would apply to this dilemma.

5. Think of a difficult situation in your life. Would you like to be used by God in this ordeal? (Be honest. Sometimes we don't want to be.) If so, how? If not, why?

6. The missionary Amy Carmichael wrote, "Often his call is to follow in paths we would not have chosen." How might unchosen circumstances shape your usefulness to God?

Esther entered the harem unprepared for its pressures, but as the story unfolds she grows in character and usefulness to God. When we step into his service we can feel inadequate, even baffled. But God uses who we are, where we are, and develops our character as we yield to him.

BELIEVING IN WHO YOU CAN BE

The New Testament speaks of qualities that reflect God's character within us. We can pray that God will develop these qualities in us so we can serve him better.

Look up the following Scriptures and read them aloud.

- Galatians 5:22–23
- 2 Peter 1:5–7

King James/ Philip 4:11

The leader will assign each woman one or more qualities mentioned in these verses. Then each woman can pray that group members will develop a specific characteristic in their lives. (If the group is small, the leader may need to assign more than one quality to each woman.) One woman can then conclude the prayer time by offering the group to God for his use.

THE GREAT CHARACTER HUNT

Ralph Waldo Emerson said, "The best effect of fine persons is felt after we have left their presence." This week, learn from women who could have a lingering effect on you.

With a friend: Rent and watch a video about a famous woman or literary character. Discuss the traits that led to her success or downfall. What lessons can you learn from her to apply to your lives?

On your own: Think of a woman whom you admire. What spiritual qualities does she possess? Write out a character description of this woman, underlining the qualities in her that you'd like to emulate. Keep this description and use the underlined words as a prayer list. If it's appropriate, send a copy of the description to the woman and thank her for being who she is.

YOUR WAY, HIS WAY

"For my thoughts are not your thoughts, neither are your ways my ways," declares the LORD. "As the heavens are higher than the earth, so are my ways higher than your ways and my thoughts than your thoughts."

—Isaiah 55:8–9

2/17/04

Listen Up

*Influence grows by consulting
the right sources.*

*E*sther pulled back a curtain and squinted at the dusky courtyard below her bedroom window.

"I wish I could see as far as the palace gates. I wish I could see Mordecai at his usual post. But even when it's daylight I can't see that far," she said to herself and the trusted messenger waiting just inside the boudoir door. "Are you sure it was him sitting there, in sackcloth and ashes? He's a strong and reserved man. That doesn't sound like him."

"Yes, my queen," said the messenger, bowing his head. "He beats his chest and cries loudly."

"Then go to him tonight and ask what is wrong. Tell him that Esther his kin wants him happy. Take a fine robe and explain that his queen has sent royal clothes for her beloved subject to wear. But be discreet."

When the door silently closed behind her confidant, Esther fell across the bed, face down and trembling.

Such strange behavior for Mordecai. If I could make him stop mourning perhaps the trouble would disappear, she thought, pushing a foreboding spirit from her. *But he is like a father to me, and I'd never command him to do something. He wouldn't listen anyway. Not if it's something that important.*

She turned over and stared at the silk folds in the canopy. *But do I really want to know?* She pushed the anxious thoughts from her mind, and soon fell asleep.

When a familiar knock sounded at the door, the young queen woke abruptly. She groped across the unlit room and pulled the door ajar.

"It's not good news for Mordecai and your people," the messenger whispered.

Esther straightened her back and ushered him into the room. "If it's for them, I can stand anything," she said. "Light a candle and explain why my cousin weeps."

WHOM CAN YOU TRUST?

Esther had a trusted adviser in her life. Mordecai told her the truth and offered his support during difficulty. But what about you? Do you have trusted advisers? People to whom you can explain yourself, listen to their counsel, and trust that they keep your best interest in mind? If not, it's time to pray about finding some for your life.

As you pursue God and his path you need to gather around friends, family, and acquaintances who can counsel you with spiritual wisdom. Some may interact with you daily, others only occasionally — whatever fits your needs and circumstances. These advisers can include the following:

- *Admonishers* who warn you when you're heading offtrack.
- *Celebrators* who believe in your destiny and applaud the journey.
- *Encouragers* who strengthen your spirit and resolve.
- *Intercessors* who pray with and for you, and wage spiritual warfare on your behalf.
- *Mentors* who personally or professionally have traveled the road ahead of you and share their wisdom.
- *Planners* who help you map the future and make decisions.
- *Counselors* and therapists who assist you through personal dilemmas.

Before meeting together this week, evaluate your life and list or briefly describe the types of advisers you need. Then write an overall *realistic* description of the qualities these people should possess. (Remember: Nobody will match the abilities of a Superman or Superwoman.) Begin asking God to bring these advisers into your life, both through your initiation and his divine encounters.

Financial —
Planners — make decisions about my work
Counselors - getting through the emotions of divorce

ADVICE FOR THE AGES

Esther's reign swiftly becomes threatened by the self-centered decisions of two careless leaders. But amidst the chaos she listens to wise counsel from a trusted adviser and prepares for a spectacular risk. What advice would motivate a queen to risk her life — advice that still inspires women today? The answer lies in today's discussion.

Before you begin the discussion, read the Bible text, Esther 3–4.

1. Haman's ancestors the Amalekites swore enmity against the Jews. God had ordered the Jews to "blot out the memory of Amalek from under heaven" (Deuteronomy 25:17–19), but they didn't follow through on his command. Considering this and other possible factors, what could be Mordecai's motivation(s) for refusing to bow to Haman in 3:1–4?

   Because he (Mordecai) was a Jew & God was the only one he should bow down

2. Even before Haman consults the king, he asks magicians to cast lots for the day the Jews would be exterminated. Then he approaches the king with his plan. Read verses 7–10. What does the king's response reveal about his relationship with Haman and his approach to ruling the kingdom?

   Haman was boasful about how rich he was & how many sons he had & how he had been promoted to high office

3. According to verses 12–15, what is particularly cruel about the king's edict to kill the Jews?

4. Esther 4:9–11 indicates that Esther doesn't know about the edict, but she quickly understands the consequences of an attempted intervention. (See the Behind the Scenes section, "Consider the Consequences," on page 41.) Why would even the queen be subject to the gold scepter's whims?

5. Verses 12–14 express Mordecai's poignant advice to Esther. Why would he believe that "relief and deliverance for the Jews will arise from another place" (verse 14) if she doesn't act?

6. Esther heeds the advice of her cousin and then declares a fast (verses 15–16) before she approaches the king. Why would she do this? Also read Isaiah 58:6–12 for insight. How would a fast be another form of listening to advice?

Maybe be in constant prayer

7. What additional qualities has Esther developed that make her a woman God can use?

patient, obedient

Behind the Scenes

CONSIDER THE CONSEQUENCES

Esther, when the gravity of the situation has dawned upon her, at first resists Mordecai's instruction to appeal to the king on behalf of her people. Her reasons are given in [chapter 4] verse 11. It comes as something of a surprise to us, but the new queen who so enraptured Xerxes when he first saw her — and could still do so, as the next chapter will show — has not been called to his presence for a month. Here as in other matters we are not told why.

The reasons for Esther's hesitations are clear enough, however. The structure of Persian authority set some store by inaccessibility of the king to any except those whom he chose to call to him. The seven princes of 1:14, who "saw the king's face," occupied a specially privileged position. Infringement on the etiquette by which the king's face was veiled from all others was tantamount to an act of treason. And to enforce the ban upon the over-bold, a squad of men armed with axes stood about the throne ready to hack them down unless the king in his mercy extended the golden scepter to restrain them.

Esther's anxiety, therefore, was not misplaced.

— J. G. McConville, *Ezra, Nehemiah, and Esther*

THE POWER OF LISTENING

These chapters in Esther's story exemplify the power of <u>listening</u> to the
<u>right people</u>. Esther listens to the advice of Mordecai and then to God
during a fast. In turn, Mordecai heeds his adopted daughter's instruc-
tions. Both must listen to each other via messengers. As they consider
each other's words they grow in faith, courage, and resolve.

1. As you focus on becoming a woman God can use, what could be the
    value of listening to advice? What could be the pitfalls?

    strengthen your relationships with God
    a new way or value of an idea
    we need to be sure that God is the
    ultimate decision maker
    If it (the decision is not made in love

    Prov. 19:27

2. How can you prepare yourself for listening to advice? Consider the
    actions, cautions, qualities, and attitudes to cultivate.

    Pray to God first & be of a teachable
    spirit - look up scriptures & that
    it is the Gospel

3. How might you determine the appropriate people to listen to?

    Ask God to lead you to the right
    person - a person who is fruitful
    & happy people

In quietness *Isaiah*

4. Once you've heard advice, how can you judge whether it's wise or applies to you? Develop five criteria for filtering the input you receive. Write them on a whiteboard or easel pad so everyone can see them.

30:15
1:10
3

1. scripture for support
2. fasting + praying
3. seeing the many ways the Lord gives us *message*
4. praying for peace

5. Mordecai's words "for such a time as this" can still stir women's hearts today. Why would this be so? Do they hold particular meaning for you? Explain your response.

God preparing events to be at a particular time

Like Esther, when we listen to advice we're faced with decisions. Will we believe, follow, change? Will we risk? These questions follow the counsel of people, but most of all, they accompany a relationship with God. How will you answer?

Prayer Matters

ASKING FOR GOD'S ADVICE

Begin your group prayer time with this litany, then each woman can ask God for specific advice and wisdom about making a difference in her world for him. Conclude with the last two lines.

Leader: Lord, you said if we ask, we will receive.
Group: Lord, please hear our prayers.
Leader: God, you said if we ask, you will give us wisdom.
Group: God, please hear our requests.
All: So now we seek your advice.

(Each woman asks God for advice about her situation.)

Leader: Father, we thank you for hearing our prayers.
All: And we believe you will answer us. Amen.

CULTIVATE YOUR LISTENING SKILLS

Seeking advice means cultivating your listening skills. This week listen — really listen — to women who will share their wisdom with you.

With a friend: Have coffee with a friend and conduct an advice-giving session. Both of you can bring a list of "Decisions I Need to Make," explaining each situation or decision and asking for the other person's input. Before you begin, agree that neither of you has to follow through on the other's counsel; you are only gathering information. However, you may discover that your friend's advice is wise indeed!

On your own: Interview a few spiritual women you trust, asking, "How do you know when you've heard God's voice? How do you recognize the advice he's giving to you?" Consolidate their answers and look for similarities. What can you learn from them?

Words to Remember

THE LISTENING EAR

Listen to advice and accept instruction,

and in the end you will be wise.

Many are the plans in a man's heart,

but it is the LORD's purpose that prevails.

— Proverbs 19:20–21

The Big Move

*Being spiritually useful
means taking risks.*

3/2/04

*E*sther leaned toward the mirror and with the tip of a manicured fingernail wiped a speck of wayward color from her upper lip. Tilting her head right and then left, she asked a waiting servant, "How do I look?"

The woman held out the queen's celebrated robes to suggest urgency. "More beautiful than ever, my queen. Come, put on your royal mantle for your visit with the king."

Esther nodded.

For a moment they gripped hands, then the servant clasped and adjusted Esther's robes in silence. She followed her quiet queen into the barren hallway and spread the outer garment's splendor across the cold floor. As the servant straightened the garment, a mournful groan rose from within.

"Are you certain you want to do this, Queen Esther?" sobbed the servant. "Remember what happened to Vashti!"

Esther could not, dared not, look back.

"Vashti's fate is always with me," she said gently. "But I can't forget Mordecai's words. Perhaps I am the woman for such a time as this; perhaps I am not . . ." Esther paused and shifted under the weight of emotion. "If I remain silent my position will not protect me from the law. Eventually I will be slaughtered, just as my people will be. I would rather die with the honor of attempting to save them than the disgrace of being found out later."

"Then may the gods be with you." The servant kneeled as Esther moved forward, the magnificent train stirring behind her.

"Yes, may Yahweh be with me," echoed the queen.

WHAT'S YOUR RISK FACTOR?

What feelings does the word *risk* conjure up in you? Exhilaration? Fear? Resentment? Joy? A combination of these? In your journal or on other pages write your answers to these questions before you meet with the group.

- How do you feel about risk? Why?

  sometimes scary

- What is the greatest risk you've taken in your life? What was the outcome? How did you feel about it?

  Coming through my divorce

- What risk might God be prompting you to take now? How do feel about it?

  to go ahead with my life + my business

Ask God to prepare you for the risk he's asking you to take as — just like Esther — you become a woman he can use.

THE ROYAL RISK-TAKERS

Scripture falls silent about Esther's three-day fast, but she emerges strengthened to act on her words, "If I perish, I perish" (4:16). She has become a risk-taker. But even without knowing it, so have other characters in this tension-building story. Haman and Mordecai also risk their lives in a royal roulette.

Who will win? Only those vying for something greater than themselves.

Before you begin the discussion, read the Bible text, Esther 5–6.

1. In 5:2–3, what would motivate the king to spare Esther and extend such a lavish offer? Speculate on several possibilities, then pinpoint which is the most likely reason.

   Very confidently - unafraid comely, Wisely not confrontationsly

2. Esther didn't articulate her concerns to the king immediately. Instead, she staged two banquets for him and Haman to attend (verses 4–8). Do you think Esther entertained the men twice because she was (a) afraid to act, (b) stalling for time, (c) plotting to cleverly humiliate Haman, or (d) trying to beguile the king first? Discuss the varying opinions.

   She has been waiting on Gods timing

3. In verses 9–14, Haman exposes more of his despicable character. His wife isn't sterling either. What couple(s) in history would you compare them to? Why?

Bonnie & Clyde

4. In 6:1–3, why would the king order the chronicles of his reign to be read to him? Explore the obvious and not-so-apparent reasons. Also consult the Behind the Scenes section, "The Hidden God," on page 49.

The king wanted to hear again of Mordecai's good deed. as God had wished

5. In verses 4–6, why would the king present his question to Haman as a riddle rather than name the person he wants to honor? What does Haman's response in verses 6–9 indicate about his perceived relationship with the king?

He was very humiliated & embarrassed

6. In verses 12–14, Haman senses the impending doom. Why would his wife and friends think he won't win against Mordecai?

Behind the Scenes

THE HIDDEN GOD

Though God's name isn't mentioned in the book of Esther, his presence permeates the pages. Many gods existed in the multicultural Persian empire, with their names recorded in official documents relating to each people group. The Jews, however, followed only one God, so a story about them assumed that they worshiped Yahweh.

As Esther's saga unfolds, "coincidences" occur that point to the providence and detailing of a "hidden" God who protects his people. So far we've witnessed these events:

- Mordecai raises his orphaned cousin Esther (2:7).
- Esther, one of God's chosen people, enters the harem (2:8).
- The chief eunuch favors her (2:9).
- Of all the beautiful women, Esther is chosen as queen (2:17).
- Mordecai hears of a conspiracy and saves the king's life (2:21–22).
- Xerxes reads a book that recalls Mordecai's deed (6:1–2).
- The king spares Esther and offers her anything she desires (5:2–3).

Through their words and actions, Esther and Mordecai also point to an omnipresent God.

- Mordecai won't bow to anyone other than Yahweh (3:2).
- He believes that even without Esther's intervention, God will save his people through other means (4:14).
- Fasting denotes supplication to God (4:16).

In the remaining chapters, watch for more ways that a God behind the scenes acts on behalf of his people, in concert with two cousins' willingness to risk all for him.

7. In these chapters, do you observe any additional qualities that make Esther a woman God can use? If so, what are they?

Sharing Your Story

FEEL THE FEAR AND DO IT

Most people, when faced with risk, feel some degree of fear. So what's the difference between those who risk and those who don't? The ability to "feel the fear and do it anyway."

Some fears can be exposed as unfounded or irrational. We can squash them. Other fears are realistic to the situation, and we need God's strength to move ahead. Spend the rest of this session evaluating how to get beyond your fears and step toward his plan for you.

1. We each measure risk differently. Review the list below, asking every woman to rate each activity as "high risk," "moderate risk," or "low or no risk." Then compare notes. What opinions do you share in common? Where do you differ? In practical ways, how can you respect one another's different perceptions about risk?

- Skydiving from a plane. *high*
- Cooking a new recipe for company. *mod.*
- Moving across country to a new home. *low*
- Changing jobs. *mod.*
- Speaking in front of a large group. *high*
- Explaining your faith to a nonbeliever. *low*
- Changing hairstyles. *No*
- Dating as an adult. *low*
- Starting up a business or ministry. *mod*
- Acting on what you believe God has told you. *No*

2. What qualities are needed to be a risk-taker? Why?

faith & confidence
Knowledge & relationship in God
II Corinthians
12:9

3. What do you fear about risk-taking? Why? Write a collective list on the whiteboard or easel pad.

fear of failure
the unknown

4. Risk and loss walk hand in hand. You could lose everything to gain what you desire. Or you may need to lose some things to find others. Create a list of criteria for determining whether what you gain from a risk is worth what you will lose. List both the spiritual and practical aspects. For example: "It's worth the loss if I gain a deeper walk with God." Or, "It's worth the pain if I gain the fulfillment of the dream buried in my heart."

James 1: 2-8

The Dream Giver

5. Look at the list of fears again (#3). Which are unfounded and unrealistic? Cross them out. Discuss how, practically and spiritually, you can overcome the remaining ones.

Life presents many challenges, but the most important center on the question, "Will you lose your life to save it?" Esther asked herself this, and stepped forward. It's a question for you, too, especially if you desire usefulness to God.

MOVING TOWARD RISK

Use your "fear list" as a point of prayer for your group. Name the risk you feel called by God to take and an accompanying fear that you feel. Then have the group gather around you, praying against the fear and for the risk. Conclude with thanksgiving to God for his coming strength and direction.

THINK BIG, START SMALL

When broken into incremental steps, risk doesn't seem so daunting. This week "start small" and take a few nonrisky steps toward a big-risk goal.

With a friend: When you're considering a risk or involvement, it's wise to count the cost before you begin. With a friend sample something that you'd like to do, but aren't sure about. Serve in a soup kitchen once, visit the college campus and gather up admissions paperwork, talk heart-to-heart with the people at an organization you want to join, or stop at an art store and estimate what it will cost to renew a painting career.

Soak in your friend's encouragement and observations. Whatever the risk, it's easier when shared by two.

On your own: Review the group's "fear list" and your own misgivings about following God's path for you. Choose one fear this week and accomplish a small task that faces it.

For example, if you dread moving away from your hometown because of a job transfer, call van lines and obtain estimates for what transporting your belongings will cost. A concrete, nonrisky step helps build your strength. Faced incrementally, a risk doesn't loom too large!

Pray Jeri.   9 ulcers on leg
for

Feb 23
Dr. Appt.

A SOULFUL DECISION

For whoever wants to save his life will lose it, but whoever loses his life for me and for the gospel will save it. What good is it for a man to gain the whole world, yet forfeit his soul? Or what can a man give in exchange for his soul?

— Mark 8:35–37

Taking a Stand

You can win over your spiritual enemies.

Esther wished she could scream.

It would calm her nerves, but it also might extricate Haman's influence that nauseated everyone he touched. She'd always loathed the man, but lately her servants complained that he'd grown especially despicable. More haughty than ever (if that were possible!) and gruesomely destroying people for no good reason, except his extreme insecurity and competitiveness.

I don't understand why Xerxes doesn't see how truly wicked Haman is, she thought.

Yesterday she had witnessed Haman's descent into evil firsthand. Beautifully dressed to please her husband, she'd swept into the banquet hall to his admiring gaze. She'd swirled and billowed her skirts, teasing the king for more approval and camouflaging her nervousness. But the performance had stopped abruptly when she glimpsed Haman's face. The lust in his eyes had chilled her. Even as they reclined at the table, she felt his disturbing gaze.

Xerxes, can't you see this? Esther had screamed inside. *Why don't you notice and punish him?* She'd turned toward Xerxes, who was fingering the wine bottles sitting on the table. She coughed softly, and the king looked up and smiled.

"Now, Esther, what is your wish? You may have up to half of the kingdom," he'd reminded her.

She'd smiled back and hesitated. *That is a vast and loving offer, but still not enough to save my people,* she thought. Then she'd heard herself inviting the men to another banquet the next day.

Now tomorrow had arrived, and Esther's stomach tightened. *Today is the day. Today is the day,* she recited. *One more meal and I'm that much closer to ... whatever the king decides.*

WHAT'S IN THE WAY?

Much like Esther, when you decide to become a woman God can use you'll soon discover obstacles standing in the way. These barriers may be people, events, circumstances, even yourself, and they extend beyond the fears discussed in the last session. To overcome these obstacles you first need to identify them.

To prepare for this week's session, gather a pen, pad, and Bible, then escape the interruptions at home — visit a park, the library, a church sanctuary — and think about these obstacles. Create a list of those originated by people, events, circumstances, and yourself. Add others you consider significant. Then strategize ways to dismantle these obstacles, one by one. But be realistic in your strategies; deconstruction requires time and patience.

Before you begin, though, ask God to reveal his strategies for their demise. From a spiritual and practical perspective, what does he require of you? What will he do? How might warfare from your unseen enemy factor into these problems? What obstacles might actually be boundaries from the Lord?

Once you've identified the true obstacles and God-directed strategies, ask him for a Scripture verse to inspire your battle against these enemies of spiritual effectiveness. Write it out, then pray about each barrier. As you move deeper into usefulness, consult and adjust your strategy list.

bad time management
being too busy

THE CLEVERNESS OF A QUEEN

Once Esther risked her life to gain the king's attention, her responsibility didn't fade. She still needed to face and defeat her people's enemy. This required more faith and courage, but also strategy and persistence. Today's session uncovers how clever and creative a determined young queen can be!

Before you begin the discussion, read the Bible text, Esther 7–8.

1. Begin by reading Esther 7:1–2 again. At the second banquet, why would Esther wait until the king asked about her request?

   perfect timing - undivided attention. She had the wisdom & patience for the correct timing

2. When Esther finally traps Haman in verses 5–6, how does she describe him? Why would she choose these words?

   An evil man, enemy

3. Why does the episode in verses 7–8 further seal Haman's fate? See the Behind the Scenes section, "A Case of Bad Etiquette," on page 58 for insight. How might Esther be feeling when Haman falls before her?

   terror - fearful

4. On the same day the king awards Esther with Haman's estate and Mordecai with a signet ring. See 8:1–2. Why would Xerxes do this instead of immediately saving the Jews? What might be the significance of each of these actions?

handing over major trust

5. In verses 3–6 Esther risks again. Read about it and then discuss these questions: Why would Esther need to approach the king for this situation a second time, deferring to him as before? Do you think this risk was greater or lesser than the first time she approached the king? Explain your answer.

yes - it could be her family killed - the law couldn't be changed -

6. The king wakes up to Esther's crisis in verses 7–10 and orders Mordecai to write another decree about the Jews. Why would Xerxes ask Mordecai to write it, rather than creating the decree himself?

7. Now consult verses 11–14. Why would the Jews be required to fight against their enemies? Why would they be so joyful, not knowing the conflict's outcome?

That God would be their protector

Behind the Scenes

A CASE OF BAD ETIQUETTE

Based on the Hebrew text, it's unclear whether the terrified Haman fell on the couch or beside it next to Esther. Some translators even say the poor man "flung himself across the couch" or "huddled across the couch."

Whatever Haman did, it displayed bad etiquette. A regulation for Assyrian harems decreed that "if a courtier speaks with one of the women of the palace, he must not come closer to her than seven paces." Though Xerxes ruled a Persian court, his harem practices borrowed heavily from Assyrian customs. Drawing near any woman in his harem constituted an offense, so standing close to the queen could invoke serious consequences. Let alone flinging oneself at her!

Knowing this, it's easier to understand Xerxes' outrage toward Haman and his proximity to Esther and the infamous couch. The queen was not sitting, but reclining, as was the Persian custom. However Haman was positioned, he wasn't standing upright. The king could have mistaken Haman's action as attempted assault or rape.

Sharing Your Story

THE WEAPONS OF SPIRITUAL WARFARE

Esther's strategy to save the Jews pivoted on naming and standing against the enemy. The queen lived under Xerxes' overall protection, but when the enemy encroached, she needed to call upon his kingly resources for deliverance. Once she exposed Haman, the sovereign employed his power to stave off destruction.

ESTHER – *Becoming a Woman God Can Use*

This ancient chain of events mimics the never-ending battle in the spiritual realm. Yes, we ask God for his protection and deliverance, but we also brandish his weapons of warfare when the unseen enemy strikes. Today you'll examine how spiritual warfare assists a woman used by God.

1. Just as Esther named Haman as her enemy, we need to identify the enemies of our souls. Look up Ephesians 6:12 and 1 Peter 5:8. Who are our spiritual enemies? What is their goal? Where do we wage battle with them?

2. From your experience, how do Satan and his armies attack us? Discuss both the obvious and subtle ways he wars against us, and make a composite list on a whiteboard or paper so everyone can see it. What methods of attack had you not considered before? Are there any on the list that you need to pay special attention to? Explain.

3. According to Ephesians 6:13–18, what are our weapons for spiritual warfare? Write them on a whiteboard or paper, too. Then discuss how, in practical ways, you can incorporate these weapons into your daily lives.

4. Verses 13–14 of the Ephesians passage tell us to "stand your ground" and to "stand firm." How might the devil discourage you from standing firm as you become a woman God can use? In specific ways, how can you stand firm when the enemy attacks?

5. How can you help one another discern and fight enemy attacks?

Though the devil's attacks are real, you need not fear him. The Bible says that "the one who is in you is greater than the one who is in the world" (1 John 4:4), and Jesus reminded us, "I have overcome the world" (John 16:33). With the weapons of warfare, you can defeat spiritual enemies and confidently become a woman God can use. Make it your goal to understand and utilize spiritual warfare.

Prayer Matters

DELIVER US FROM EVIL

Divide into groups of two and pray for the spiritual obstacles in each other's lives — the barriers that keep you from being women God can use. Ask for his protection and intervention, but also wage spiritual warfare against the unseen forces that want to render you useless. Thank the Lord for his deliverance from obstacles and evil.

BLESSINGS ON YOUR HOUSE

This week, take preventive action against your spiritual enemies by asking for God's blessing and protection.

With a friend: Speak a blessing on each other's homes. Pray through every room, asking God to prosper those who live in the house. You can also anoint each room with oil, a biblical practice to symbolize God's protection. Also pray about difficulties and enemy attacks on spiritual growth and relationships. End by thanking and praising God for his blessing and protection.

On your own: Create a blessing book. In a small notebook write Bible verses about God's blessing, comfort, protection, deliverance, and weapons of spiritual warfare. Claim and pray through these promises when you feel blocked from spiritual effectiveness.

Words to Remember

GOD IS GREATER

Do not be overcome by evil, but overcome evil with good.

— Romans 12:21

Greater is he that is in you, than he that is in the world.

— 1 John 4:4 (KJV)

The Joy of Legacy

Today's decisions affect the generations.

*E*sther waved to the cheering crowds bursting through the palace gates. The beaming Xerxes stood beside her. Normally the king didn't share the spotlight with anyone, especially a woman, but there had been nothing "normal" about the last few days. Esther had saved her people, but even more, she'd driven the fear of God — and the fear for their lives — into the hearts of Persia, including his own.

Even a king like myself, who is unafraid to challenge the mighty Greeks, knows when another Sovereign is too powerful to ignore, thought Xerxes. He smiled at his wife.

Even my proud husband celebrates the victory, thought Esther, smiling back. *How could he not? Yahweh is watching.*

Suddenly the crowd pushed back to the sound of tambourines. A troop of nimble Jewish women leapt and danced in a circle, pounding their instruments and praising the Lord for his mercies. Another circle formed around them, singing the words of an ancient psalm:

Praise the LORD.
Praise the LORD, O my soul.
   I will praise the LORD all my life,
   I will sing praise to my God as long as I live.
Do not put your trust in princes,
   in mortal men, who cannot save.
When their spirit departs, they return to the ground;
   on that very day their plans come to nothing.
Blessed is he whose help is the God of Jacob,
   whose hope is in the LORD his God,
the Maker of heaven and earth,
   the sea, and everything in them —
   the LORD, who remains faithful forever.
He upholds the cause of the oppressed . . .

The crowd parted again, with a band of raucous warriors carrying Mordecai above their shoulders. They plopped the winded nobleman at Esther's feet. She laughed and helped him up, then honored him with a hug.

This is the delirious joy of Purim, thought the queen as they embraced. *May this day always be a celebration!*

Setting the Stage

WHAT WILL THEY SAY?

At the end of your life, what will people say about you? Their words will contribute to your legacy. Before you attend the last group meeting, write out what you'd like remembered about you. These questions may help:

- What did you accomplish?

- How did you spend your time?

- How did you affect other people's lives?

- In what ways did you grow personally?

- What was your relationship with God like?

- How were you used by God for his purposes?

- What have you left behind for future generations?

Through the years you can purposefully work toward this legacy of words. Keep these descriptions in a safe place and review them periodically for motivation. Like Esther's, your life can also be a cause for celebration.

Discussing Esther's Story

A CAUSE FOR MORE CELEBRATION

Even before the Jews entered battle, they celebrated their deliverance from Persian oppressors. And they've celebrated this occasion ever since. Esther's intervention left a legacy for future generations to remember, draw courage from, and be thankful for their survival as a people. Even more, the Bible reminds us all that Esther was a woman God used mightily.

Before you begin the discussion, read the Bible text, Esther 9–10.

1. In 9:1–4, the Jews prepare to fight. Verse 1 states that they "got the upper hand." The people in the provinces could still fight, so why would they allow the Jews to prevail?

2. Note how the Jews overcome their enemies in verses 5–10. Usually the victors seized the belongings of the defeated, but the passages states, "they did not lay their hands on the plunder" (verse 10 and later verses 15 and 16). What could be the significance of this omission?

3. At Esther's request (verses 13–15) the king orders the bodies of Haman's sons to be hung. Why would the queen ask for this?

4. Herodotus, a Greek historian, described Esther as "a cold and vindictive queen." If you were Esther and heard this description, how would you feel? In your heart, how might you respond to this characterization? In contrast, how would the Jews describe Esther? The people of the Persian empire?

5. Esther left a legacy to the Jewish people, celebrated in the holiday called Purim. Read about this holiday in verses 18–32 and the Behind the Scenes section, "A Party Called Purim," on page 67. Why is it important for the Jews to always celebrate this holiday? What is the significance of Esther issuing the decree for establishing Purim?

6. Think back over Esther's life. Create a timeline that chronicles her story. Draw a long, horizontal line. Below the line indicate the major events of her life. Above the line write the character traits she exhibits in relationship to those events. Review the timeline and discuss these questions: How has Esther grown in character? In her ability to be used by God?

7. In a few sentences, describe Esther's legacy to her people — and to us all.

Behind the Scenes

A PARTY CALLED PURIM

Thousands of years after Esther's life the Jews still celebrate Purim, the holiday that promotes Jewish unity. Though Purim practices vary around the world, they center on four customs:

- *Reading Esther's story.* Celebrants gather in the synagogue to hear the Purim story about Esther and the Jews' deliverance. It's customary to respond to the story's dramatic events. For example, hissing at Haman or applauding Esther.
- *Giving gifts to the needy.* Both the poor and the well-to-do contribute to a fund for those in need. Each person gives according to his or her ability, breaking down the barriers between rich and poor. The gifts are usually financial, though food can be contributed, too.
- *Sending food to new and old friends.* The minimum requirement is to give two types of food to one friend. After this, the creative combinations are endless. Friends often give food gift baskets or beautifully wrapped packages of treats.
- *Feasting and drinking.* Finally, the Purim Feast features traditional foods and plenty of wine. The meal's objective is to increase the feelings of warmth and closeness to one another.

Sharing Your Story

TODAY'S DECISIONS, TOMORROW'S MEMORIES

Would you like to leave behind a legacy worth celebrating? Like Esther, it's important to understand that your decisions today affect the future — how people will remember, be influenced by, and celebrate you.

1. Why do people want to leave a legacy? What does leaving a legacy mean to you?

2. A legacy encompasses much more than leaving behind a financial inheritance. What other aspects of our lives build a legacy? Write the ideas on a whiteboard or paper so everyone can see them. Then number the legacy aspects according to their value, with #1 as the most important, #2 as the next in importance, and so forth.

3. If part of your legacy is to be used by God, what decisions can you make today that will affect this desire's fulfillment? Add these decisions to your legacy list.

4. Your leader will pass out an index card or piece of paper. Write "God, Use Me" on one side of the card. Then write a few sentences about how you'd like to be used by God in your lifetime. Flip over the index card and write "My Legacy." With a few sentences describe the legacy you'd like to leave behind. You will use this card in the closing prayers today.

ESTHER — *Becoming a Woman God Can Use*

5. Close the discussion section by singing or reading together the hymn "Take My Life and Let It Be."

> *Take my life and let it be*
> *Consecrated, Lord, to Thee;*
> *Take my hands and let them move*
> *At the impulse of Thy love,*
> *At the impulse of Thy love.*
>
> *Take my feet, and let them be*
> *Swift and beautiful for Thee;*
> *Take my voice and let me sing*
> *Always, only, for my King,*
> *Always, only, for my King.*
>
> *Take my lips and let them be*
> *Filled with messages for Thee;*
> *Take my silver and my gold,*
> *Not a mite would I withhold,*
> *Not a mite would I withhold.*
>
> *Take my love, my God, I pour*
> *At Thy feet its treasure store;*
> *Take my self and I will be*
> *Ever, only, all for Thee,*
> *Ever, only, all for Thee.*

When you dedicate your life to God and his work in the world, you'll be used by him. You're headed toward a memorable and inspiring legacy!

Prayer Matters

LAUNCH YOUR LEGACY

To conclude your study of Esther, spend time in prayer, launching each woman into her spiritual legacy. Place a chair in the middle of the room. One by one, a group member will sit in it, with the other women standing in a circle around her.

Ask the woman to read both sides of her index card aloud. First, she can read, "God, Use Me" and second, "My Legacy." When she finishes, lay hands on the seated woman (an act of imparting blessing to her) and pray that God will honor her desires so she can leave a legacy behind for him. Pray, too, about specifics of the woman's life.

After Hours

GIFTS FOR THE GENERATIONS

Celebrate the legacies of your life! In the next weeks, honor those who have contributed to the spiritual lives of women.

With a friend: Plan a surprise Legacy Tea for an older woman (or women) in your church, neighborhood, or community who has contributed significantly to the spiritual lives of younger women. Invite women she has influenced and ask them to give testimonials, read Scripture, recite poetry, present a skit, or anything else that would celebrate the honoree's contributions. End with spontaneous prayers of thanksgiving for her.

On your own: Begin keeping a Legacy Book for a younger woman in your family. Paste in photos, mementos, and written remembrances of female relatives — their personalities, accomplishments, relationship to God, and legacies they left (or want to leave) behind. Give it to this younger woman on a special occasion, accompanied by a fun storytelling time about these memorable relatives.

Words to Remember

EYES ON THE GOAL

Therefore, since we are surrounded by such a great cloud of witnesses, let us throw off everything that hinders and the sin that so easily entangles, and let us run with perseverance the race marked out for us. Let us fix our eyes on Jesus, the author and perfecter of our faith.

— Hebrews 12:1–2

ESTHER — *Becoming a Woman God Can Use*

Leader's Guide

These guidelines and suggested answers can help enhance your group's effectiveness. However, remember that many questions require opinions rather than "right" or "wrong" answers. Input is provided only for those questions that may need additional insight.

To guide the group effectively, it helps to complete each session privately before you meet together. Then as you lead the group you can better facilitate the discussion by clarifying the questions when needed, offering suggestions if the conversation lags, drawing out members who aren't contributing much, redirecting the focus from participants who tend to dominate, and asking women for explanation when they contribute simple "yes" or "no" answers. Also, during the prayer time be sensitive to women who need encouragement or ideas for praying as a group.

For all of the sessions provide a whiteboard, chalkboard, or easel pad for making lists and comments that the entire group can observe. Also provide markers for writing.

SESSION ONE: *Who's in Control?*

Objective: To understand that despite the circumstances, God is in control.

Discussing Esther's Story: A Battle of the Wills

1. The author may have wanted to underscore the pagan atmosphere of the story. Or the magnitude of Xerxes' power. Or the opulence an unknown Jewish girl will later possess and use to save her people.
2. Since the king wanted to display his power, wealth, and solidarity, his wife's support would contribute significantly to that image.
3. Mostly the request was degrading, but perhaps Vashti also didn't want to "lose face" in front of her guests. Or it was a

power struggle between her husband and her, to show him the outrageousness of his request. Or she had grown tired of his self-centeredness.

6. Answers will vary, but remind the group that God's ways can be mysterious to us, and that he works out bad circumstances for his good.

Sharing Your Story: God in the Shadows

1. Remember to bring copies of a local newspaper to the meeting.

SESSION TWO: Wrong Place, Right Attitude

Objective: To consider the character qualities that God can use.

Discussing Esther's Story: Beauty on Parade

1. Xerxes may have missed Vashti and regretted what he did to her.
2. Mordecai could have liked living in Susa and probably had a job and privileges he didn't want to give up. He also deeply loved his cousin Esther and was devoted to her — as well as loyal to the king.
3. Mordecai may not have had a choice. Esther may have been required by law or force to enter the harem. Or perhaps Mordecai wished for his cousin to attain prominence in the kingdom, for himself and his people. Or maybe Esther wanted to enter the harem. Regarding her nationality, perhaps Mordecai instructed Esther to remain quiet because there were still prejudices against and repercussions for Jews, especially those in power.
5. Some women may not understand Esther's submissiveness to her circumstances, or they may dislike the beauty pageant approach to finding a queen — as if beauty is all that matters! They might also feel uncomfortable with the male-dominated society and the decisions of these men.
6. Answers will vary, but explain that despite our past and present circumstances, God can use us if we yield to him.

Sharing Your Story: But What About Me?

4. Bring a stack of index cards or hand-sized pieces of paper to the session.

Objective: To seek out advisers who will encourage
your usefulness to God.

Discussing Esther's Story: Advice for the Ages

1. Mordecai may be refusing allegiance to anyone but God. He
   also might be acting out an old enmity between the Jews and
   the Amalekites. He could just hate Haman. Or it's a combination of all these reasons.
2. Xerxes places an incredible amount of trust in Haman's advice.
   The king also doesn't pay close attention. He doesn't find out
   who these people really are, yet he signs away their lives.
3. The edict announces ahead of time when and how the Jews
   will be slaughtered. There is no escape, so they must live in
   horror until the assigned day of their death. Also, they are contributing members of society, now condemned to death for no
   good reason.
4. Even the queen had few rights, and the laws of the Medes and
   Persians applied to everyone. She was only to appear when he
   beckoned her.
5. Most likely Mordecai still believes that God will keep his
   covenant and spare his people, no matter the circumstances.

Sharing Your Story: The Power of Listening

5. Most of us want to know that God has created us for a special
   purpose, "for such a time as this."

SESSION FOUR: *The Big Move*

Objective: To be willing to take risks for God.

Discussing Esther's Story: The Royal Risk-Takers

1. Again, it could be her beauty. Or he may have grown to love
   Esther. He could be acting on a whim, the way he's behaved
   in other situations, or be wanting to impress people with his
   ability to make such an offer. Further still, he may not know
   why he uttered the offer, and be acting out God's plan for him.

4. The king seems to enjoy focusing on himself, or he may need to catch up on the kingdom's history. Whatever the reason, it's God's providence at work.

5. Maybe the king likes to be a bit mysterious. Or perhaps he assumes Haman knows whom he is talking about. Haman assumes that his relationship with the king is the same as always. Haman expects that all accolades belong to him, that the king will always honor him above everyone else.

6. Haman's wife and friends probably understand that the God of the Jews cannot be defeated. He avenges on behalf of his people.

SESSION FIVE: *Taking a Stand*

Objective: To recognize and wage warfare against spiritual enemies.

Discussing Esther's Story: The Cleverness of a Queen

1. Esther may be piquing the king's interest. If he asks the questions, then he's sure to be interested and feel in control.

2. Esther clearly states that Haman is vile and the enemy. The words contain shock value and uncover his hidden motives. It's also urgent that she pinpoint the source of evil immediately.

4. Xerxes seems to be a man who responds to immediate circumstances, forgetting all else. These actions also are related to his power as king. Esther now controls all that Haman worked for, and Mordecai wears the ring that seals the king's edicts. The king has placed great trust in them both.

5. (Question 1) Evidently Xerxes has forgotten to do anything about his wife's request.

6. This may be an indication of how he's shifted his trust to Mordecai. Perhaps he thought Mordecai would know best how to save his people. The king might also now be afraid of the God of the Jews.

7. The edict to kill the Jews could not be rescinded because of the country's unchangeable laws. The new decree enables the Jews to fight back and save themselves. Also, the Jews probably understood that God was on their side, and that he would

deliver them, as in past times. They know their nation's history and God's promise to preserve them if they turn to him. They had submitted to him through fasting.

SESSION SIX: *The Joy of Legacy*

Objective: To begin creating a personal spiritual legacy.

Discussing Esther's Story: A Cause for More Celebration

1. The people now feared the Jews and their power. They probably sensed that the God of the Jews would avenge the wrongs against them.
2. The Jews were fighting for ethical reasons — to save their lives and possessions. They weren't fighting to gain anything else or for selfish reasons.
3. Perhaps to underscore to the Jews that their enemies are truly dead, that the old command to kill the Amalekites has been carried out. Maybe also to warn other people not to mistreat her people.
5. The Jews needed to remember God's covenant-keeping love and mercy toward them. Perhaps when Esther issues the decree, it exhibits her power in the kingdom and the king's reverence for the new holiday.

Sharing Your Story: Today's Decisions, Tomorrow's Memories

4. Bring a stack of index cards or hand-sized papers to the session.

About the Author

*J*udith Couchman is the owner of Judith & Company, a business devoted to writing, speaking, and editing. She is the author/compiler of forty books and speaks to women's and professional groups around the country. Judith was the founding editor-in-chief of *Clarity* magazine, and has won awards for her work in book publishing, corporate communications, journalism, and secondary education. She lives in Colorado.

WOMEN OF FAITH℠

Women of Faith partners with various Christian organizations,
including Zondervan, Campus Crusade for Christ International,
Crossings Book Club, Integrity Music, International Bible Society,
Partnerships, Inc., and World Vision
to provide spiritual resources for women.

For more information about Women of Faith
or to register for one of our nationwide conferences,
call 1-800-49-FAITH.
www.women-of-faith.com

Linda Fleck
prayers for her work
issues of a person
losing her job + prayer
for the person

Frances Simantel

Pray for Sharon Flynn
future daughter in law
to accept her

2/29/04

ZONDERVAN™

GRAND RAPIDS, MICHIGAN 49530

www.zondervan.com

Charlene
needs prayers for over eating, spending, etc. control
to help Brandon with health issues
+ also for bad behavior at school

Inice
Pray for her mother who is handicap + is
still trying to drive 83 yrs old
Isabelle — pray for understanding

Annette — good praises
works for a judge Wash Co.

3/9/04
Pray Carol Bookout
grandchildren about
growing up issues
Barbara O'Hare & sisters of
Juanita Jackson   Mary Jackson